AF228470

# THE US DECISION TO DROP THE ATOMIC BOMB

BY A. R. CARSER

**CONTENT CONSULTANT**
Allan M. Winkler
University Distinguished Professor of History (Emeritus)
Miami University of Ohio

Cover image: US president Harry Truman played a key role in the decision to drop the atomic bombs.

Core Library

An Imprint of Abdo Publishing
abdobooks.com

**abdobooks.com**

Published by Abdo Publishing, a division of ABDO, PO Box 398166, Minneapolis, Minnesota 55439.
Copyright © 2022 by Abdo Consulting Group, Inc. International copyrights reserved in all countries.
No part of this book may be reproduced in any form without written permission from the publisher.
Core Library™ is a trademark and logo of Abdo Publishing.

Printed in the United States of America, North Mankato, Minnesota
052021
092021

Cover Photo: Bettmann/Getty Images
Interior Photos: Everett Collection/Newscom, 4–5; World History Archive/Newscom, 6, 43; Red Line
Editorial, 9; AP Images, 12–13; Bettmann/Getty Images, 18–19; Tu Olles/Shutterstock Images, 21;
akg-images/Newscom, 24, 31; U.S. Navy/AP Images, 26–27, 45; Olinchuk/Shutterstock Images, 29;
George Skadding/The LIFE Picture Collection/Getty Images, 34–35; Agentur Voller Ernst/Picture
Alliance/ZB/Newscom, 37; Harry Harris/AP Images, 40

Editor: Maddie Spalding
Series Designer: Ryan Gale

**Library of Congress Control Number: 2019954302**

**Publisher's Cataloging-in-Publication Data**

Names: Carser, A. R., author
Title: The US decision to drop the atomic bomb / by A. R. Carser
Description: Minneapolis, Minnesota : Abdo Publishing, 2022 | Series: Atomic bomb perspectives |
       Includes online resources and index
Identifiers: ISBN 9781532192692 (lib. bdg.) | ISBN 9781098210595 (ebook)
Subjects: LCSH: Nuclear warfare and history--Juvenile literature. | Nuclear weapons information,
       American--Juvenile literature. | Atomic bomb--Juvenile literature. | Military history--Juvenile
       literature.
Classification: DDC 940.5425--dc23

# CONTENTS

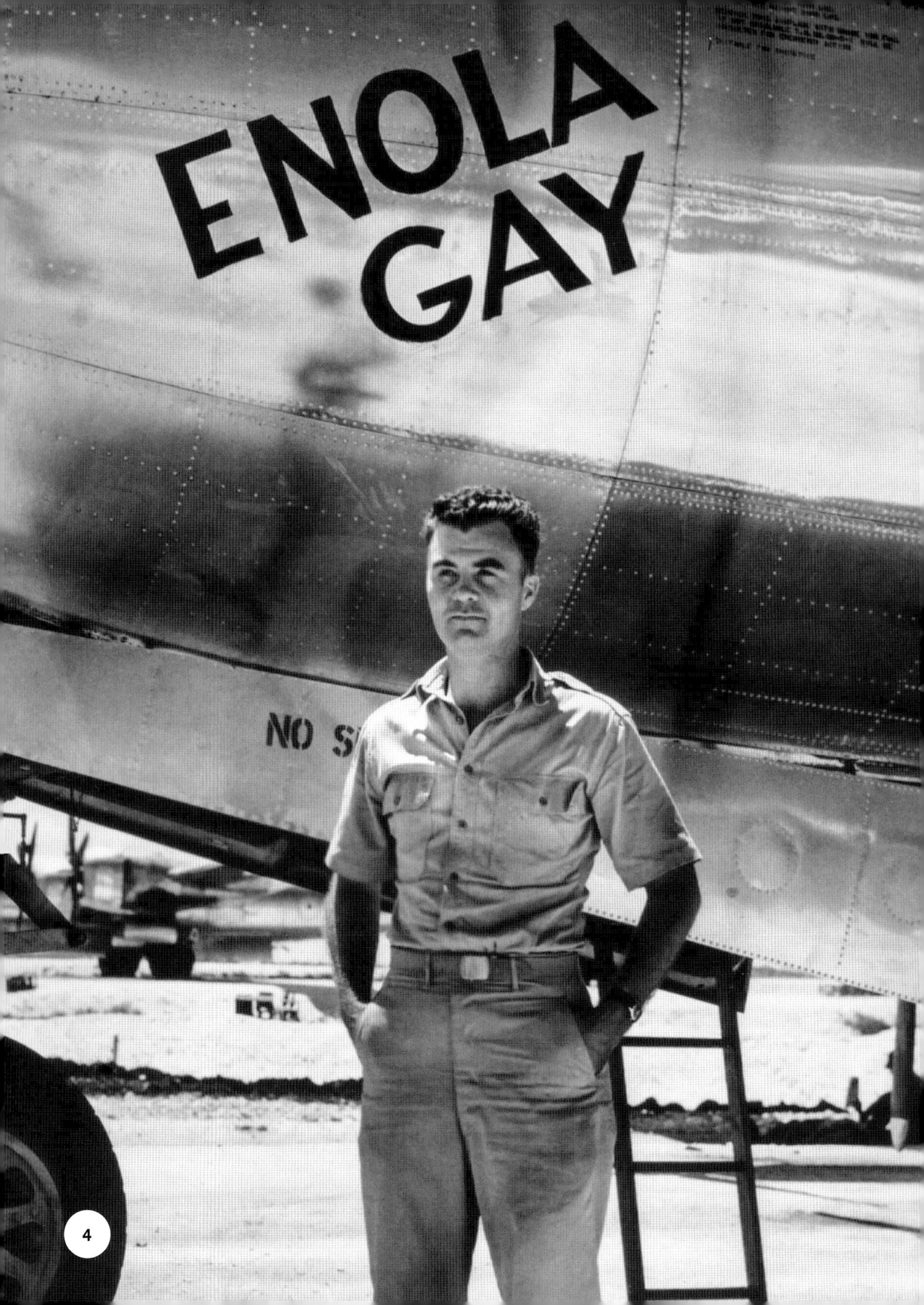

ENOLA
GAY
NO S

# A FATEFUL DECISION

"Here it comes," said George "Bob" Caron. The date was August 6, 1945. Caron was the tail gunner of the *Enola Gay* B-29 bomber plane. He sat at the back of the plane. His job was to fend off enemy attacks. He was warning pilot Colonel Paul Tibbets that a shock wave was coming. The shock wave was from Little Boy. Little Boy was an atomic bomb. Tibbets had just dropped the bomb over the Japanese city of Hiroshima.

Colonel Paul Tibbets named the *Enola Gay* after his mother.

A large plume of smoke arose from Hiroshima as fires broke out after the bomb was dropped.

The shock wave hit the plane as it flew away. The crew felt the impact. But the airplane could handle it. Tibbets flew the plane back over Hiroshima. The crew saw only black smoke.

Tibbets had prepared for this day for nearly a year. But scientists had been working on the bomb even longer. In 1942, President Franklin D. Roosevelt approved the creation of the bomb. Scientists then began developing two types of atomic bombs. One bomb was made using plutonium. Little Boy was made using uranium. It was the first atomic weapon to be used in war.

Atomic bombs are very powerful. They use the energy within an atom to create an explosion. The effort to build the first atomic bomb was called the Manhattan Project. The project began in June 1942. Scientists and military personnel across the

United States worked on it. Many people hoped an atomic bomb would end World War II (1939–1945).

## THE WAR IN THE PACIFIC

World War II was a conflict between the Allied and Axis powers. The Allied powers included the United States, Great Britain, and the Soviet Union. France and China were also among the Allies. Germany, Italy, and Japan made up the Axis powers.

By April 1945, US troops had reached the Japanese island of Okinawa. Okinawa is approximately 350 miles (560 km) south of the Japanese mainland. The Battle of Okinawa began on April 1. The fighting lasted 12 weeks. More than 12,000 US soldiers were killed. And more than 90,000 Japanese soldiers died. That was 90 percent of Japan's forces on the island. Despite its losses, Japan still had an army of 2 million men.

By May 7, 1945, Germany was no longer a threat. Germany surrendered on that day. The conflict in

# LAST MAJOR BATTLES IN THE PACIFIC

| Location | Date of Battle | Number of Soldiers Killed |
|---|---|---|
| Saipan, Mariana Islands | June–July 1944 | 3,000 US soldiers<br>29,000 Japanese soldiers |
| Leyte, Philippines | October–December 1944 | 3,504 US soldiers<br>65,000 Japanese soldiers |
| Iwo Jima, Japan | February–March 1945 | 7,000 US soldiers<br>19,962 Japanese soldiers |
| Okinawa, Japan | April–June 1945 | 12,000 US soldiers<br>90,000 Japanese soldiers |

The United States and Japan fought four major battles in the last year of World War II. This table shows the locations and dates of these battles. It also shows the number of soldiers that were killed on both sides. Which battles were most deadly? How do you think the loss of lives affected people both in the United States and in Japan?

Europe was over. But Allied troops were still fighting against Japan in the Pacific.

Most US military experts agreed that Japan had lost the war. But the Japanese refused to surrender. Many US leaders thought dropping an atomic bomb on

Japan was the best solution to try to end the war. They thought this would force Japanese officials to surrender.



## PERSPECTIVES

### PILOT PAUL TIBBETS

*Enola Gay* pilot Paul Tibbets led bombing missions in Europe during World War II. In 1944, military officials asked him to lead a special group. The group of flight crews trained to drop large bombs over Japan. Tibbets had come to terms with dropping bombs over cities and towns. On his first bombing run over Europe, he had realized that some of the people hurt by the bombs were civilians. But he decided to concentrate on his missions, not on the aftermath. He also thought bombing was the only way to force Japan to surrender.

## TRUMAN'S DECISION

In early 1945, Harry S. Truman was Roosevelt's vice president. Roosevelt never told Truman about the Manhattan Project. Roosevelt suddenly died in April. Military officials then told Truman about the bomb.

Scientists tested the first atomic bomb in the New Mexico desert on July 16.

By then, Truman had come to a decision. He thought
the US military should use the weapon against Japan.
He believed this was the best way to end the war with
minimal US casualties.

On July 26, the Allies gave Japan a choice. They
told Japan to surrender or face total destruction.
They did not mention the atomic bomb. If Japan did not
surrender, the United States planned to drop the bomb.

Japan did not surrender. So on August 6, Tibbets
flew the *Enola Gay* toward the Japanese mainland. He
released Little Boy over Hiroshima. Three days after
that, the US military dropped a second atomic bomb
over Nagasaki, Japan. The world would never be
the same.

# ROOSEVELT'S PERSPECTIVE

**A**tomic research in the United States began before the Manhattan Project was formed. A letter from scientist Leo Szilard in October 1939 spurred Roosevelt to action. Szilard described Germany's efforts to develop an atomic weapon. If successful, Germany could use the weapon on the United States and its allies. Szilard urged Roosevelt to fund US atomic research. Famous scientist Albert Einstein signed the letter.

Roosevelt, *middle*, gave a speech on January 20, 1945, after he was elected for a fourth term as US president.

Roosevelt took immediate action. He formed the Advisory Committee on Uranium. This committee was made up of scientists and government officials. It gave $6,000, which is equivalent to more than $100,000 today, to the University of Chicago. The school used this money to build the first US nuclear reactor. Scientists used this device to create a nuclear chain reaction. A nuclear chain reaction occurs when an atom is split. Neutrons from the atom hit other atoms. The neutrons split the other atoms. This process releases a massive amount of energy.

From 1939 to 1941, university laboratories did most of the atomic research. Roosevelt did not fully understand the technology's potential for destruction. Still, atomic research remained one of his priorities.

## THE MANHATTAN PROJECT

In mid-1941, Roosevelt learned Germany was making advances in its atomic weapons research. This confirmed Szilard's concerns. In response, Roosevelt formed the Top Policy Group. The group was made up of government officials and a few scientists. It would decide how to proceed with atomic research.

Through most of 1941, the United States had not yet entered World War II. But on December 7, 1941, the Japanese bombed a US Navy base in Pearl Harbor, Hawaii. After the attack, the United States declared war on Japan. It joined the Allied forces.

Atomic research became more urgent after the United States entered the war. Roosevelt ordered the Army Corps of Engineers to assist with this research. The US government created the Manhattan Project.

Roosevelt had once been the assistant secretary of the US Navy. He served in this role during World War I (1914–1918). Now he led the country through a second world war. He remembered the losses from the previous war. More than 320,000 US soldiers had died or been injured. Roosevelt supported anything that would reduce the number of American deaths in World War II.

## CHOOSING A TARGET

In September 1944, Roosevelt met with British prime minister Winston Churchill. They talked about the development of the atomic bomb. They agreed that this project should remain a secret. Both leaders thought Japan should be the target of the completed bomb.

Roosevelt did not live to see the use of the bomb or the end of the war. On April 12, 1945, he died. Truman became president. The ultimate decision to drop the bomb lay with him.

## EXPLORE ONLINE

Chapter Two discusses Roosevelt's support of US atomic research. The article below goes into more depth on this topic. Does the article answer any questions you had about Roosevelt's views?

## FRANKLIN D. ROOSEVELT

abdocorelibrary.com/decision-to-drop

# THE CASE FOR THE BOMB

When Truman took office, the Manhattan Project was in its final stages. Scientists, military leaders, and government officials met over the next four months. They discussed using the bomb to end the war. Most believed this was a wise decision.

## FIVE OPTIONS

By the summer of 1945, Truman had to decide how to end the war with Japan. He had

Truman, *left,* was sworn in as president just two hours after Roosevelt's death on April 12, 1945.

five options. One option was to continue to firebomb Japan. The United States had been bombing Japan since 1942. The bombs the US military used caused fires wherever they were dropped. The fires damaged cities and killed many Japanese people. But the Japanese refused to surrender. Truman did not think more firebombing would change their mind.

US officials also considered a blockade or an invasion. A blockade would involve US Navy ships. The ships would try to keep resources from entering Japan. But this would put many troops in danger. It would also take a lot of time. Some people thought an invasion of Japan was a better option. But an invasion could lead to a huge loss of life on both sides.

Another option was to demonstrate the bomb's power. The US military could drop the bomb over an unpopulated area. This option would not kill or injure anyone. But some advisors thought this would not be enough to force Japan to surrender.

Truman had one other option. The US military could drop the bomb on Japan. Military officials carefully chose potential targets. They sought out places that had naval ports and air bases. They also considered towns or cities that had military factories. These factories built weapons. The destruction of these factories would be a major blow to Japan. But the people who worked in these factories were civilians. They and their families lived in homes near the factories. Using the bomb on a military target would also kill civilians.

# MILITARY SUPPORT

In the spring of 1945, General Leslie Groves created the Target Committee. Groves oversaw the Manhattan Project. His committee was made up of other people who worked on the project. They included military officials and scientists. They advised Truman on how to use the bomb.

The Target Committee suggested Hiroshima as a possible target. Hiroshima was a naval port. It also had military factories. Approximately 330,000 people lived in the city.

Hiroshima was surrounded by hills. The hills would contain the bomb's destruction within the city. The committee also recommended the city of Kokura as a target. Kokura was home to one of Japan's largest stores of weapons and ammunition.

## POLITICAL SUPPORT

On May 2, 1945, Henry L. Stimson created the Interim Committee. Stimson was the secretary of war. His committee included politicians and scientists who worked on the Manhattan Project. They gave advice on where and how to drop the bomb.

## HENRY L. STIMSON

Henry L. Stimson served as secretary of war for both Roosevelt and Truman. He worked with Groves to coordinate the Manhattan Project. Like Groves, Stimson believed the atomic bomb should be used against Japan. But he did not think it was right to bomb cities without warning. However, he later changed his mind. He stood behind the Interim Committee's recommendation to drop the bomb without warning. He also defended the attacks on Hiroshima and Nagasaki.

James Byrnes was a former lawyer and congressman.

James Byrnes headed the committee. Byrnes was the US secretary of state. He thought using the bomb would minimize US deaths. He also believed this was the only way to get Japan to surrender.

The Interim Committee recommended that the atomic bomb be dropped on a populated area. It thought the bomb should be dropped without warning. This would make the biggest impact on the Japanese people. The committee believed this attack would force Japan to surrender.

# STRAIGHT TO THE
# SOURCE

In May 1945, the Target Committee wrote to Groves. Scientist Joyce C. Stearns was on this committee. He chose potential targets for the bombs. The committee explained:

*Stearns . . . surveyed possible targets possessing the following qualifications: 1) they be important targets in a large urban area of more than three miles [4 km] diameter, 2) they be capable of being damaged effectively by a blast, and 3) they are likely to be unattacked by next August. . . .*

*Hiroshima—This is an important army depot . . . in the middle of an urban industrial area. It is . . . such a size that a large part of the city could be extensively damaged.*

Source: *The Manhattan Project: The Birth of the Atomic Bomb in the Words of Its Creators, Eyewitnesses, and Historians.* Edited by Cynthia C. Kelly, Black Dog & Leventhal Publishers, 2007. pp. 319, 321.

## CHANGING MINDS

Imagine you are a member of the Target Committee who disagrees with the decision to drop the bomb. How would you try to change the minds of other people on the committee? Make sure to explain your opinion. Include facts and details that support your argument.

# ALTERNATIVES TO THE BOMB

**M**ost scientists, military leaders, and government officials supported the use of the bomb. But others cautioned against it. Some advisors recommended an invasion or conventional bombing, such as firebombing. Others supported dropping the bomb on an unpopulated area. And some officials suggested a naval blockade of Japan.

**Roosevelt, *right*, talks with General Douglas MacArthur, *left*, in 1944. MacArthur wanted to invade Japan.**

# THE INVASION OPTION

On June 21, 1945, the United States won the Battle of Okinawa. General Douglas MacArthur and Admiral Chester W. Nimitz had led the invasion of Okinawa. They made plans to invade the Japanese island of Kyushu. They called this plan Operation Olympic. After this operation, military officials planned to invade the country's main island, Honshu. They wanted to take over the capital city of Tokyo. These invasions could be one way to end the war.

MacArthur and Nimitz thought these invasions could end the war by December 1946. They estimated that there would be approximately 100,000 US casualties. Still, the men believed these invasions would kill fewer people than dropping the atomic bomb. But many US leaders did not think invasions would be enough to force Japan to surrender. Truman doubted that this option would save US lives. He also did not think it would end the war quickly.

# MAP OF
# JAPAN

US military officials considered invading the island of Kyushu. Then the military could attack Tokyo on the island of Honshu. This map shows where these places and other key locations are in Japan. Japan is smaller than the state of California. How do you think the war affected the entire country?

# THE FRANCK REPORT

On June 11, 1945, a group of scientists sent a report to the Interim Committee's Scientific Panel. The scientists worked on the Manhattan Project at the University of Chicago's Metallurgical Laboratory (Met Lab). Nobel Prize–winning scientist James Franck headed the group. Szilard was also part of the group.



The Met Lab played an important role in the development of the atomic bomb. Met Lab scientists worked in secret. They built the world's first nuclear reactor. But over time, the scientists lost influence with military and government officials. The scientists were concerned that Truman would only hear the advice of these officials. They wanted Truman to take their advice into consideration too.

The scientists' report to the Interim Committee was called the Franck Report. It warned that dropping the bomb on Japan would put the United States at risk. At the time, the United States was the only nation in the world that had an atomic bomb. But the scientists believed

other nations would soon have the technology to make these bombs. It would be difficult to keep this technology a secret if the bomb was dropped on Japan. Enemies that developed atomic bombs could target the United States. Atomic bomb attacks could destroy US society.

In the Franck Report, the scientists recommended a demonstration of the bomb. They recognized that this method might not work. In that case, they said the United States should ask for approval from its allies before using the bomb. The report urged the United

States to share the responsibility for using atomic weapons with its allies. The scientists believed this was the only way to prevent atomic warfare in the future.

On June 21, the Interim Committee met. The Scientific Panel discussed the Franck Report. At first, the panel was in favor of the demonstration. It wanted to avoid a loss of life. But the panel eventually changed its mind. It was not confident a demonstration would convince Japan to surrender. Panel members agreed a direct attack was the only option.

# STRAIGHT TO THE
# SOURCE

The Franck Report explained the consequences that could occur if an atomic bomb was dropped on Japan. It warned:

> *Nuclear bombs cannot possibly remain a "secret weapon" at the exclusive disposal of this country, for more than a few years. . . . Within ten years other countries may have nuclear bombs, each of which, weighing less than a ton, could destroy an urban area of more than ten square miles [26 sq km]. In the war to which such an [arms] race is likely to lead, the United States . . . will be at a disadvantage compared to the nations whose population and industry are scattered over large areas.*
>
> Source: *"The Franck Report." Atomic Heritage Foundation*, 2019, atomicheritage.org. Accessed 8 Oct. 2019.

## CONSIDER YOUR AUDIENCE

Adapt this passage for a different audience, such as your friends. Write a blog post conveying this same information for the new audience. How does your post differ from the original text and why?

# TRUMAN'S PERSPECTIVE

**B**efore Truman made his decision, he spoke with many advisors. These advisors included Henry Stimson and James Byrnes. On June 1, 1945, Byrnes told Truman about the Interim Committee's recommendation. He explained the group's belief that dropping the bomb was the best strategy.

Truman, *left*, gave Stimson, *right*, the Distinguished Service Medal in 1945 to honor his service to the United States.

## THE TRINITY TEST

On July 16, Truman was in Berlin, Germany. He was preparing for the Potsdam Conference, which was set to begin the next day. This was a meeting with Allied leaders. But Truman's mind was also on a desert in Alamogordo, New Mexico. At a site code-named "Trinity," scientists were testing the first atomic bomb.

The Trinity test was successful. Truman shared this news with Winston Churchill. Truman told Soviet Union leader Joseph Stalin that the United States had tested a powerful weapon. He did not say it was an atomic bomb. But Stalin knew about the bomb. Soviet spies had learned about the Manhattan Project.

## THE POTSDAM DECLARATION

The United States, Great Britain, and China issued a statement on July 26. Their statement was called the Potsdam Declaration. The Soviet Union did not take part in the statement. It had not decided whether it wanted to declare war on Japan.

Truman, *right*, stands alongside Stalin, *left*, at the Potsdam Conference.

In the Potsdam Declaration, the countries threatened Japan. They called for Japan's surrender. Japanese leaders did not respond to the declaration.

On July 30, Truman learned two atomic bombs would be ready by early August. Truman still believed bombing was the best way to end the war.

During World War II, the Japanese military captured approximately 4,120 Americans. These people were considered prisoners of war (POWs). Some were soldiers. Others were nurses or civilians. The Japanese also captured US allies, including British and Filipino soldiers. The Japanese military held these soldiers in camps. Japanese soldiers had invaded islands across the Pacific. Many of the POW camps were on these islands. The captors mistreated and starved the POWs. Four out of every ten American POWs died. Truman wanted to end the war quickly to save the lives of both US soldiers and POWs.

Other US leaders supported this decision. It was time to move forward.

## THE BOMBINGS

The morning of August 6 was sunny in Hiroshima. Then at 8:15 a.m., everything changed. Little Boy exploded above Hiroshima in a blinding flash. The ground reached 5,400 degrees Fahrenheit (3,000°C). People near the blast site died instantly. Within minutes, 90 percent of the people within 0.5 miles (0.8 km) of the blast were killed. Approximately 70,000 people died.

Emperor Hirohito of Japan learned about the attack more than 11 hours later. He urged Japan's political leaders to surrender. But they resisted. So the United States prepared to drop the second atomic bomb. The US military called this bomb Fat Man.

On the morning of August 9, a US military plane flew over Kokura. This city was the military's original target. But clouds covered Kokura. The bombers could



# PERSPECTIVES

## PUBLIC OPPOSITION

By August 7, 1945, news of the Hiroshima bombing had spread around the world. Some Americans were happy the bomb had been dropped. They thought the bomb would quickly end the war. Others were saddened and concerned by the news. Before the Nagasaki bombing on August 9, Truman received a note from Samuel McCrea Cavert. Cavert was a Protestant church leader. He begged the president to stop bombing Japan. Truman sent a reply on August 11. He stood by his decision. However, he did not wish to use any more bombs. He ordered that no more atomic bombs be dropped.

not see well enough to drop the bomb. So they flew to the secondary target, Nagasaki. There was an opening in the clouds. The bombers dropped Fat Man over the city. Approximately 40,000 people died in the attack.

On August 10, 1945, Japan surrendered to the Allied powers. World War II was finally over. Dropping the bombs had saved thousands of American lives. It might have saved many Japanese lives too. Thousands more Japanese people could have died if the United States had invaded Japan. Still, most of the people who died from the atomic bombs were civilians. Thousands more died later from illnesses caused by exposure to radiation. The final death toll was approximately 135,000 people. No one can know how history might have turned out if different decisions about the bombs had been made. The legacy of the bombings remains a complicated one.

## FURTHER EVIDENCE

Chapter Five discusses Truman's decision to drop the atomic bomb. What was one of the main points of this chapter? What evidence is included to support this point? Read the article at the website below. Does the information on the website support the point you identified? Does it present new evidence?

### HARRY S. TRUMAN'S DECISION TO USE THE ATOMIC BOMB

abdocorelibrary.com/decision-to-drop

# IMPORTANT DATES

**June 1942**
The US military creates the Manhattan Project.

**April 12, 1945**
President Franklin D. Roosevelt dies. Harry S. Truman is sworn in as president of the United States.

**May–June 1945**
Truman appoints an Interim Committee to review potential military actions to end World War II. The committee recommends that the US military drop an atomic bomb on a populated area in Japan.

**July 16, 1945**
The first atomic bomb is tested in New Mexico. The test is successful.

**July 26, 1945**
The Allied powers issue the Potsdam Declaration. In this statement, they demand Japan's surrender. Japanese officials do not reply.

## August 6, 1945

The *Enola Gay* drops the first atomic bomb on Hiroshima, Japan.

## August 9, 1945

The US military drops a second atomic bomb on Nagasaki, Japan.

## August 10, 1945

Japan surrenders, ending World War II.

### Surprise Me

Chapter Three discusses Truman's options to end World War II. After reading this book, what two or three facts about the decision to drop the atomic bomb did you find most surprising? Write a few sentences about each fact. Why did you find each fact surprising?

### Dig Deeper

After reading this book, what questions do you still have about the decision to drop the atomic bomb? With an adult's help, find a few reliable sources that can help you answer your questions. Write a paragraph about what you learned.

### Say What?

Studying history can mean learning a lot of new vocabulary. Find five words in this book you've never seen before. Use a dictionary to find out what they mean. Then write the meanings in your own words, and use each word in a new sentence.

## Take a Stand

Truman decided to use the atomic bomb against Japan
rather than demonstrate its power in an unpopulated area.
Do you think this decision was the right one to make? Or
would you have chosen a different way to end the war?
Explain your answer in a few sentences.

# GLOSSARY

**ally**
a nation that supports another nation during a war

**atom**
the smallest individual part that makes up a substance

**casualty**
someone who is injured or killed in a conflict

**civilian**
someone who is not a member of a country's military

**industrial**
relating to manufacturing or another type of business

**neutron**
a particle inside an atom

**nuclear**
relating to an atom's nucleus, or the central part of an atom

**oppress**
to control or rule over people in a harsh and cruel way

**petition**
a formal, written request to an official

**radiation**
the waves of energy sent out by sources of heat or light, or by radioactive material such as that from a nuclear bomb

**urban area**
an area in or near a city

# ONLINE RESOURCES

To learn more about the US decision to drop the atomic bomb, visit our free resource websites below.

Visit **abdocorelibrary.com** or scan this QR code for free Common Core resources for teachers and students, including vetted activities, multimedia, and booklinks, for deeper subject comprehension.

Visit **abdobooklinks.com** or scan this QR code for free additional online weblinks for further learning. These links are routinely monitored and updated to provide the most current information available.

# LEARN MORE

Conley, Kate. *World War II through the Eyes of Franklin Delano Roosevelt*. Abdo Publishing, 2016.

Murray, Laura K. *World War II Technology*. Abdo Publishing, 2018.

# INDEX



## About the Author

A. R. Carser is a freelance writer who lives in Minnesota. She enjoys learning and writing about history, culture, and society.